DOT-FTA-MA- 26-7071-03-1
DOT-VNTSC-FTA-03-06

U.S. Department
of Transportation
**Federal Transit
Administration**

Materials Investigation of Thermal Triggers Used in Pressure Relief Devices on Transit Buses

July 2003
Final Report

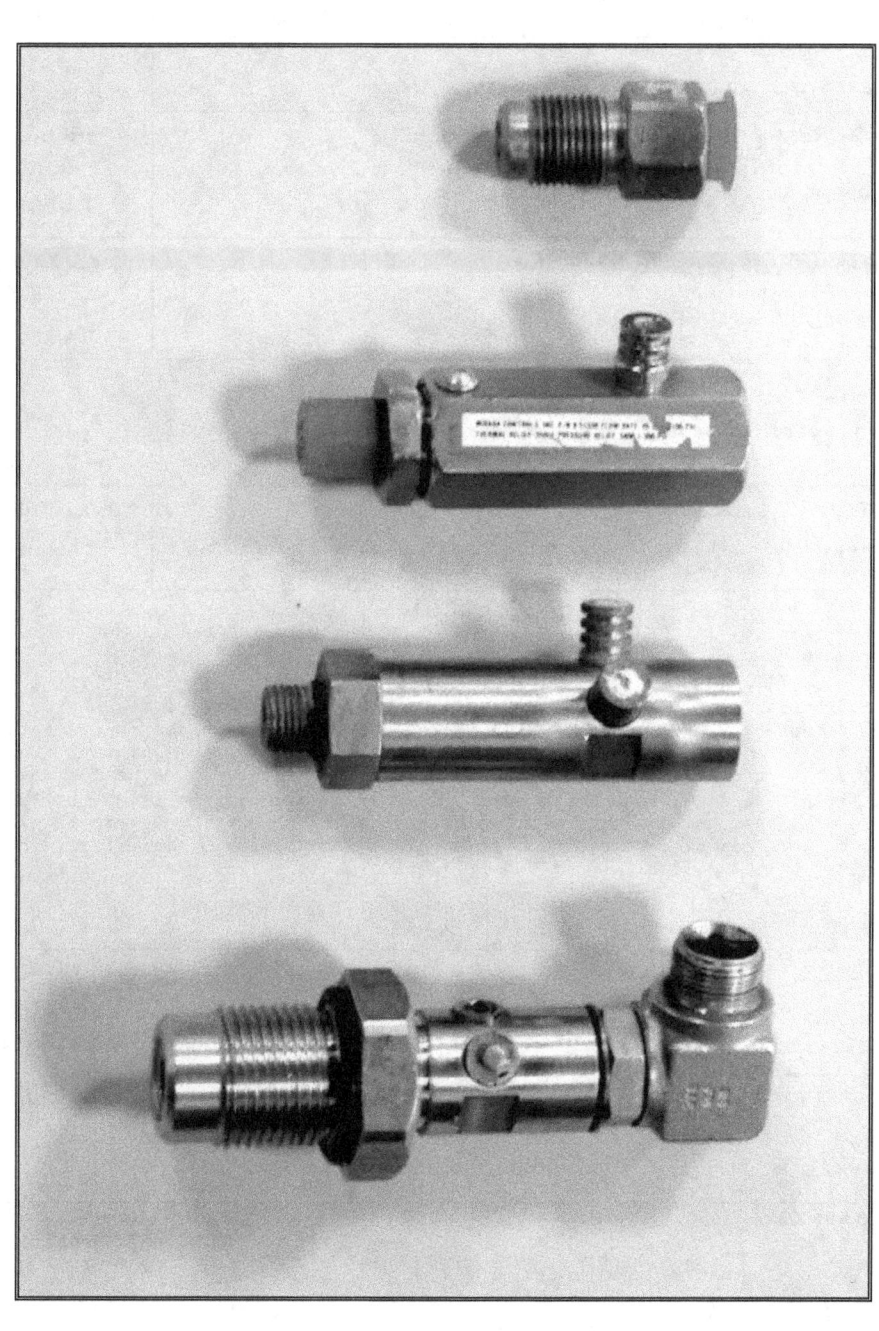

REPORT DOCUMENTATION PAGE		Form Approved OMB No. 0704-0188

The public reporting burden for this collection of information is estimated to average 1 hour per response, including the time for reviewing instructions searching existing data sources, gathering and maintaining the data needed, and completing and reviewing the collection of information. Send comments regarding this burden estimate or any other aspect of this collection of information, including suggestions for reducing this burden, to Washington Headquarters Services Directorate for Information Operations and Reports, 1215 Jefferson Davis Highway Suite 1204, Arlington, VA 22202-4302, and to the Office of Management and Budget, Paperwork Reduction Project (0704-0188), Washington, DC 20503.

1. AGENCY USE ONLY (Leave blank)	2. REPORT DATE June 2003	3. REPORT TYPE AND DATES COVERED Final Report – July 2003

4. TITLE AND SUBTITLE	5. FUNDING NUMBERS
Materials Investigation of Thermal Triggers Used in Pressure Relief Devices on Transit Buses	TT-383 U3077
6. AUTHOR(S) Nathan Rolander*/**, Douglas Matson** , William P. Chernicoff*	

7. PERFORMING ORGANIZATION NAME(S) AND ADDRESS(ES)	8. PERFORMING ORGANIZATION REPORT NUMBER
*Volpe Center **Tufts University Dept. of Mechanical Engineering Cambridge, MA 02142 Medford, MA 02155	DOT-VNTSC-FTA-03-06

9. SPONSORING/MONITORING AGENCY NAME(S) AND ADDRESS(ES) U.S. Department of Transportation Federal Transit Administration Office of Research, Demonstration and Innovation	10. SPONSORING/MONITORING AGENCY REPORT NUMBER FTA-MA-26-7071-03-2

11. SUPPLEMENTARY NOTES This work was performed under contract to:	U.S. Department of Transportation Volpe National Transportation Systems Center Cambridge, MA 02142

12a. DISTRIBUTION/AVAILABILITY STATEMENT This document is available to the public through the National Technical Information Service, Springfield, VA 22161	12b. DISTRIBUTION CODE

13. ABSTRACT (Maximum 200 words)

This investigation pertains to the composition and general condition of the thermally activated trigger mechanism of Pressure Relief Devices [PRD's], safety devices used on compressed natural gas cylinders commonly used to store fuel on transit buses. These trigger mechanisms provide the essential function of the PRD, and any problems with the trigger will result in poor device performance.

The report analyses the condition of the eutectic material used in the triggers, its composition, condition, and any flaws that may occur. Following the experimental investigation, failure criterion for the triggers were computed based on observed flaws in the trigger material. These computations provide a measure of the reliability of the triggering devices, and thereby of their effectiveness.

14. SUBJECT TERMS Pressure Relief Device, Natural Gas Safety, Alternative Fuel, Bus Safety			15. NUMBER OF PAGES 33
			16. PRICE CODE

17. SECURITY CLASSIFICATION OF REPORT Unclassified	18. SECURITY CLASSIFICATION OF THIS PAGE Unclassified	19. SECURITY CLASSIFICATION OF ABSTRACT Unclassified	20. LIMITATION OF ABSTRACT

NSN 7540-01-280-5500

Standard Form 298 (Rev. 2-89) Prescribed by ANSI Std. 239 18 298-102

NOTICE

This document is disseminated under the sponsorship of the U.S. Department of Transportation in the interest of information exchange. The United States Government assumes no liability for its contents or use thereof.

NOTICE

The United States Government does not endorse products or manufacturers. Trade or manufacturers' names appear herein solely because they are considered essential to the objective of this report.

Metric/English Conversion Factors

English to Metric | Metric to English

LENGTH (Approximate)

English to Metric	Metric to English
1 inch (in) = 2.5 centimeters (cm)	1 millimeter (mm) = 0.04 inch (in)
1 foot (ft) = 30 centimeters (cm)	1 centimeter (cm) = 0.4 inch (in)
1 yard (yd) = 0.9 meter (m)	1 meter (m) = 3.3 feet (ft)
1 mile (mi) = 1.6 kilometers (km)	1 meter (m) = 1.1 yards (yd)
	1 kilometer (km) = 0.6 mile (mi)

AREA (Approximate)

English to Metric	Metric to English
1 square inch (sq in, in^2) = 6.5 square centimeters (cm^2)	1 square centimeter (cm^2) = 0.16 square inch (sq in, in^2)
1 square foot (sq ft, ft^2) = 0.09 square meter (m^2)	1 square meter (m^2) = 1.2 square yards (sq yd, yd^2)
1 square yard (sq yd, yd^2) = 0.8 square meter (m^2)	1 square kilometer (km^2) = 0.4 square mile (sq mi, mi^2)
1 square mile (sq mi, mi^2) = 2.6 square kilometers (km^2)	10,000 square meters (m^2) = 1 hectare (he) = 2.5 acres
1 acre = 0.4 hectare (he) = 4,000 square meters (m^2)	

MASS-WEIGHT (Approximate)

English to Metric	Metric to English
1 ounce (oz) = 28 grams (gm)	1 gram (gm) = 0.036 ounce (oz)
1 pound (lb) = 0.45 kilograms (kg)	1 kilogram (kg) = 2.2 pounds (lb)
1 short ton = 2,000 pounds (lb) = 0.9 tonne (t)	1 tonne (t) = 1,000 kilograms (kg) = 1.1 short tons

VOLUME (Approximate)

English to Metric	Metric to English
1 teaspoon (tsp) = 5 milliliters (ml)	1 milliliter (ml) = 0.03 fluid ounce (fl oz)
1 tablespoon (tbsp) = 15 milliliters (ml)	1 liter (l) = 2.1 pints (pt)
1 fluid ounce (fl oz) = 30 milliliters (ml)	1 liter (l) = 1.06 quarts (qt)
1 cup (c) = 0.24 liter (l)	1 liter (l) = 0.26 gallon (gal)
1 pint (pt) = 0.47 liter (l)	
1 quart (qt) = 0.96 liter (l)	
1 gallon (gal) = 3.8 liters (l)	
1 cubic foot (cu ft, ft^3) = 0.03 cubic meter (m^3)	1 cubic meter (m^3) = 36 cubic feet (cu ft, ft^3)
1 cubic yard (cu yd, yd^3) = 0.76 cubic meter (m^3)	1 cubic meter (m^3) = 13 cubic yards (cu yd, yd^3)

TEMPERATURE (Exact)

English to Metric	Metric to English
$[(x - 32)(5/9)]$ F = y C	$[(9/5)y + 32]$ C = x F
$(x + 460)/1.8$ = y K	$(y \times 1.8 \text{ B } 460)$ = x F

PRESSURE (Exact)

English to Metric	Metric to English
1 psi = 6.8948 k Pa	1 M Pa = 145.04 psi

ENERGY & ENERGY DENSITY (Exact)

English to Metric	Metric to English
1 Btu = 1.05506 kJ	1 MJ = 947.81 Btu
1 Btu/lb = 2.326 kJ/kg	1 MJ/kg = 430 Btu/lb

QUICK FAHRENHEIT-CELSIUS TEMPERATURE CONVERSION

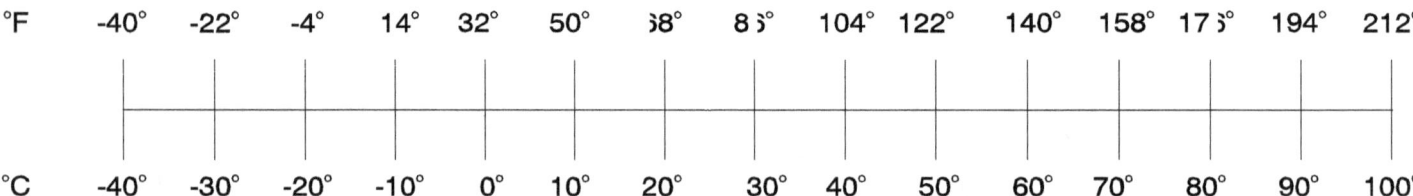

°F	-40°	-22°	-4°	14°	32°	50°	68°	85°	104°	122°	140°	158°	176°	194°	212°
°C	-40°	-30°	-20°	-10°	0°	10°	20°	30°	40°	50°	60°	70°	80°	90°	100°

I. Table of Contents -

II. List of Figures -

III. Document Nomenclature -

III.a Acronyms -

PRD	-	Pressure Relief Device
CNG	-	Compressed Natural Gas
DAQ	-	Data Acquisition
SCXI	-	Signal Conditioning and Switching Interface

III.b Definitions -

Eutectic Composition -
A specific alloy composition which solidifies at a lower temperature than all other alloy combinations.

Metal Creep -
Progressive deformation of a metal or alloy over a period of time. The process occurs via diffusion within the material. This time dependant strain is caused by a constant load or stress, particularly at elevated temperatures.

Plastic Deformation -
Permanent deformation of a material caused by continued applied stress exceeding the materials yield strength.

Abstract

This investigation pertains to the composition and general condition of the thermally activated trigger mechanism of Pressure Relief Devices (PRD's). PRDs are safety devices on compressed natural gas cylinders, commonly used to store fuel on transit buses. These trigger mechanisms provide the essential function of the PRD, and any problems with the trigger will result in poor device performance.

The report analyses the condition of the eutectic material used in the triggers, its composition, condition, and any flaws that may occur. Following the experimental investigation, failure criteria for the triggers were computed based on observed flaws in the trigger material. These computations provide a measure of the reliability of the triggering devices, and thereby of their effectiveness.

1. Background

Pressure Relief Devices (PRDs) are standard equipment on all compressed natural gas containers. The function of a PRD is to vent the compressed natural gas in the case of a fire, preventing rupture and the subsequent high-pressure gas release with a possible ignition and explosion. Compressed natural gas is stored at a maximum settled pressure of 3600 psi. If the gas is released at high-pressure in certain environments, the result could be catastrophic. Therefore, PRD design and manufacture must be of very high quality. The PRD must offer a degree of protection and reliability that meets or exceeds that of the cylinder in order to provide the proper degree of safety. The PRDs under this investigation are used on CNG cylinders for transit busses. They came under scrutiny beginning in the early 1990s, when many malfunctions occurred, where the natural gas vented. The importance of having reliable components is increasing with the shift towards alternative fuels, and especially compressed hydrogen-powered vehicles. Because hydrogen storage cells would see even higher pressures and temperature ranges, the performance of today's compressed natural gas vehicles may serve as the performance benchmark.

A primary goal of the study described in this report was to find evidence of material creep or plastic deformation. Creep phenomena have been blamed for previous PRD failures; however, to date no evidence supports this assumption, since trigger material in the PRD is not exposed to high cylinder pressure. The analysis determined the physical condition of the PRD by disassembly and dissection, including metallography and thermal profiling. The results obtained provided insight into the functionality of the PRDs and possible causes of failure.

Metallurgical analysis of contemporary PRDs was performed by the Tufts University Mechanical Engineering Department for the U.S. DOT/RSPA/Volpe National Transportation Systems Center. Previous PRD failure studies have not fully identified the failure modes and mechanisms. Without proper failure mode identification a satisfactory solution cannot be implemented. There are currently around 6,200 natural-gas-powered transit buses in the United States. During a 1997 study of 703 buses, a total of 132 gas release events were recorded, resulting in one serious fire. In December 2000, another unintentional release resulted in a deflagration. The calculated frequency of release is between 0.0013 - 0.0358 per bus per year. Since that time, releases and failure rates have decreased but still occur. This investigation was conducted in two phases; engineering analysis of the physical and metallurgical aspects of the failed PRD's, and statistical analysis to support the engineering results and detect failure patterns.

2. The Pressure Relief Device

The PRD investigated is a Mirada PRD, Serial Number 10416. This PRD was in service at Metro Regional Transit, Akron, Ohio, in 2000 when a PRD of the same design failed during a fueling. It was later shipped to the Volpe Center for investigation. It was chosen as a specific study tool to represent other PRDs in transit service. While design and manufacturing processes differ between PRDs used in transit service, the similar materials and principles of operation allow for a general application of the lessons learned. The PRD was used with a Type IV compressed natural gas container. Type IV containers use composite materials to form the structural part of the cylinder, and as such are lighter and stronger than traditional steel containers. However, composite materials are more susceptible to heat, particularly open flame, requiring faster venting of the gas in a fire. For this reason Type IV PRDs employ a thermally activated trigger mechanism to release the gas, as opposed to the more simple melt-away plug used on steel containers. This mechanism complexity creates more potential failure modes.

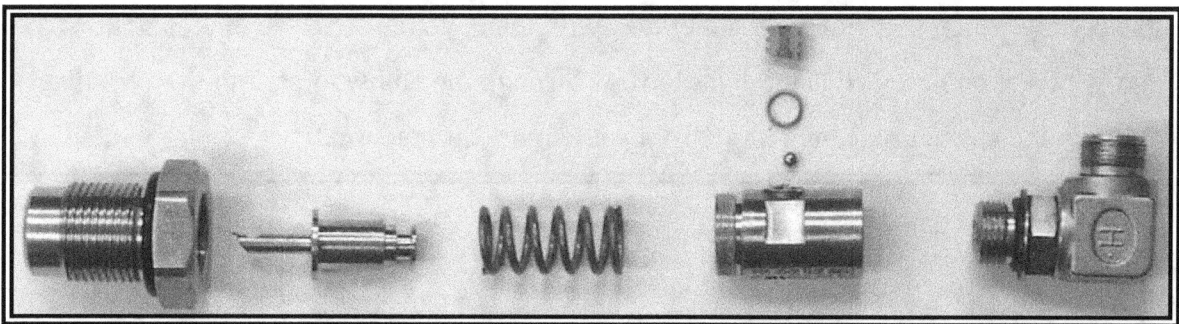

Fig 2.1 - Exploded Mirada PRD Photograph

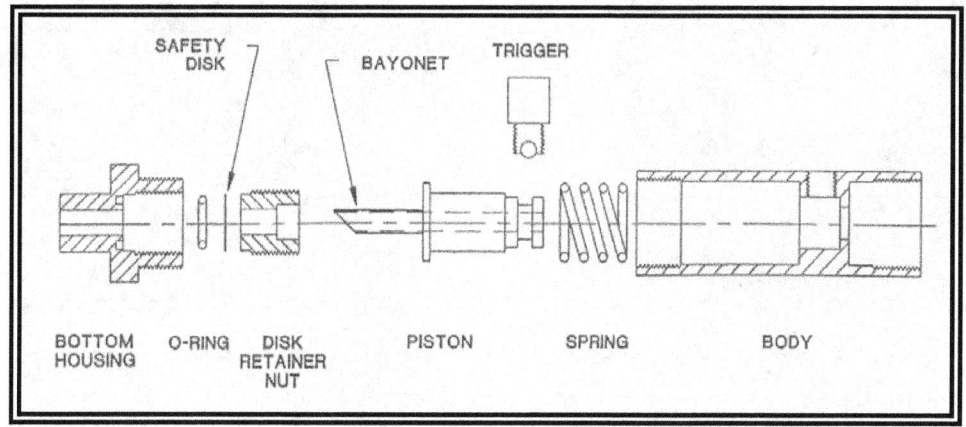

Fig 2.2 - Exploded Mirada PRD Schematic

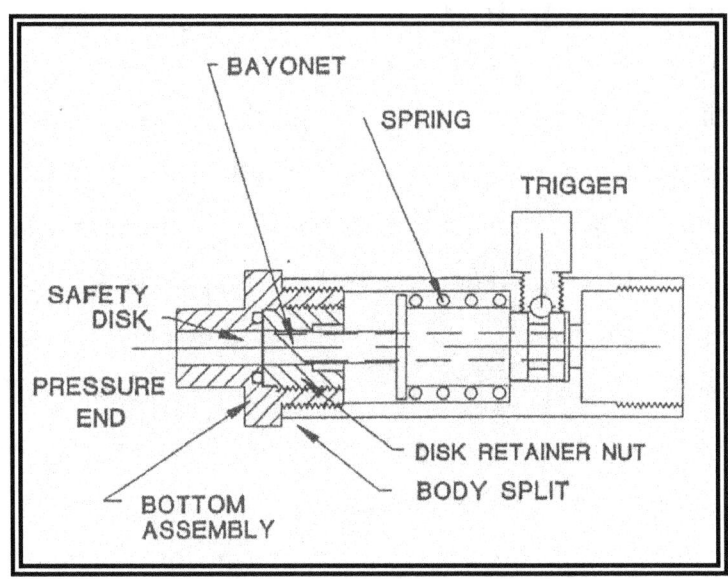

Fig 2.3 - Assembled Mirada PRD

Mirada PRD components and assembly are shown in Figs 2.1 - 2.3. The trigger mechanism is a eutectic alloy that melts, allowing the ball bearings to move and releases the spring, which punctures the safety disk with the bayonet. This bayonet is hollow, allowing the compressed natural gas to flow through the elbow joint, into the vent tube moving the gas to a safe area away from passengers (not pictured).

Fig 2.4 - Pressure Disk in place (left) and punctured with bayonet (right)

3. Triggering Device

The thermally activated triggers are the critical component to the Mirada PRDs functionality. These two triggers secure a ball bearing each that fits in the notched ring in the bayonet, securing it in place. This trigger arrangement is shown in Fig 3.1. The triggers consist of a brass outer section with concentric circular fins, surrounding a eutectic material in the center. This brass outer section contracts halfway up from the

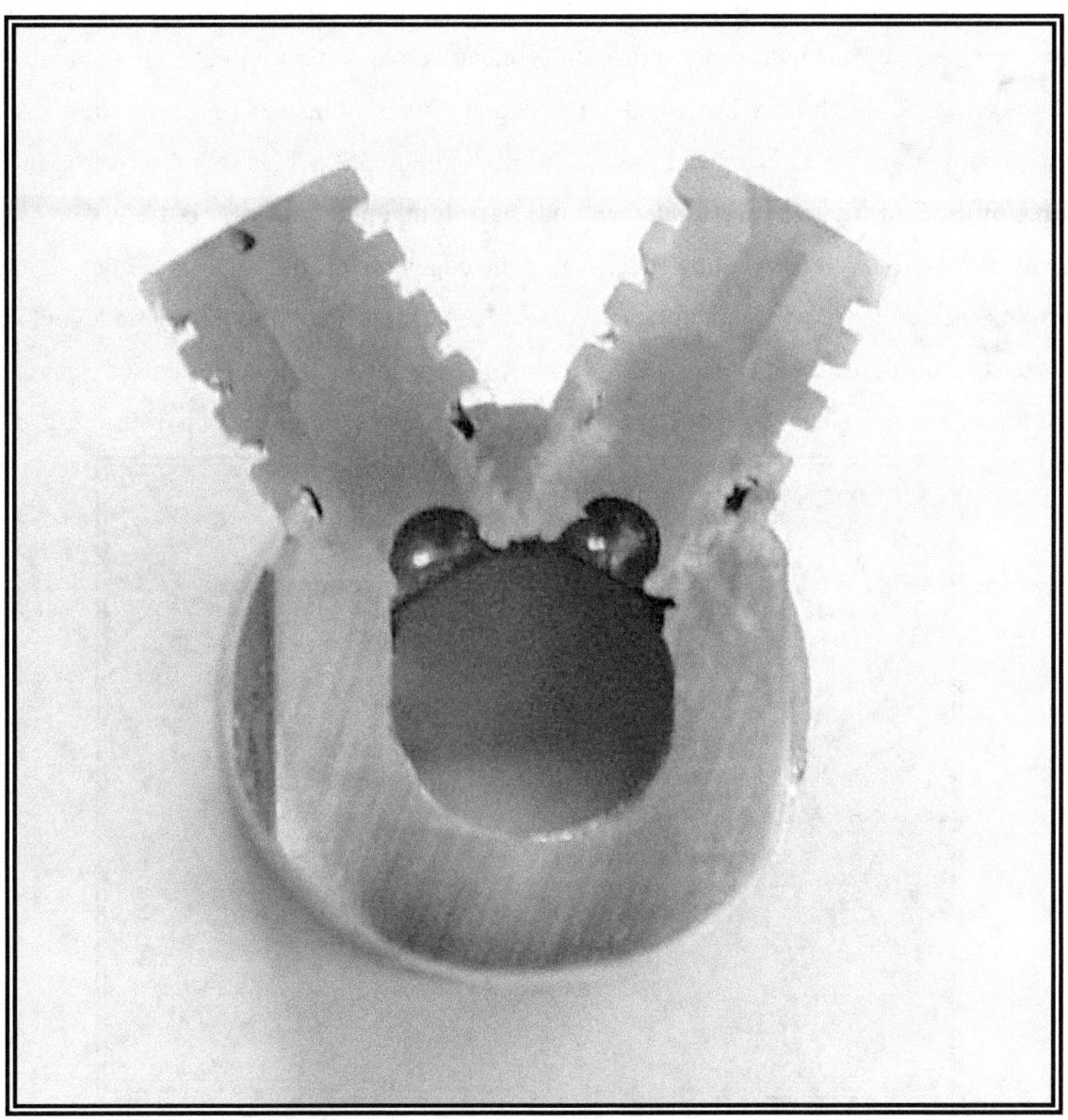

Fig 3.1 - Sectioned View of Mirada PRD, ball bearings removed

bottom, containing the ball bearings after the eutectic material melts. The bottom of the brass shafts are threaded and lock into the main mild stainless steel PRD body sealed with metal washers to ensure a tight seal.

The surface of the eutectic material exposed to the atmosphere is coated with a spot of paint, which is intended to help the bus maintenance crews identify PRD triggers experiencing deformation. However, Fig 3.1 shows that no deformation has occurred in this trigger. The surface of the eutectic is flush with the surface of the brass casing.

The eutectic alloy specified is 55.5% Bismuth, 44.5% Lead, with 255°F (123.8°C) as its melting point. Any deviation from this eutectic composition will change the melting characteristics, which were investigated in Section 5. Visual inspection of the triggers showed a void in the eutectic near the top surface (Figure 3.2). This was discovered in three of the four triggers investigated and has been found previously by Battelle Consulting Group. It is a casting flaw, where the edges cool faster than the center, leaving the center liquid. As the liquid cools and solidifies, it contracts, leaving a void in the cast. This defect could be avoided if a hot-plug casting technique were used, leaving the top of the cast eutectic to cool last and creating a depression in the top of the cast.

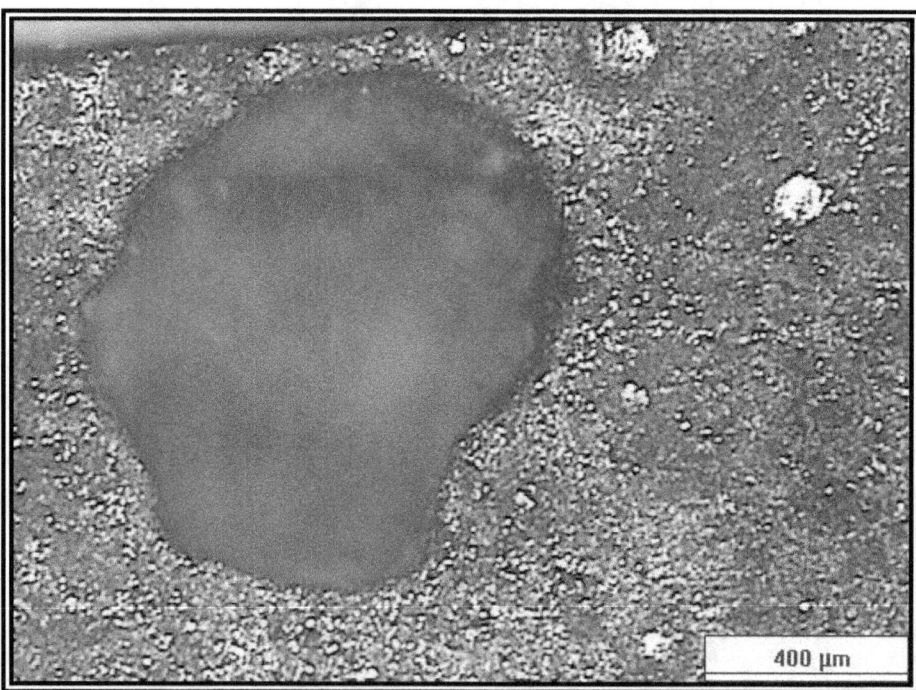

Fig 3.2 - Void in eutectic material near top surface under microscope

4. Metallography

The analyzed section of the PRD was made by using a lathe to face off the stainless steel body and outer brass casing until the eutectic core was exposed. During the machining operation the part was drenched with coolant to keep the temperature low to avoid phase change in the eutectic material, which would ruin the part for analysis. Care was taken to prevent material pull-out. After the casing was removed, the section was ground down with a 600 grit carbide polishing disc to clear away the machining marks. The polishing disc was continually flooded with water to avoid temperature change. The final step was to polish the surface with a 5 micron polishing suspension on a polishing pad. This process left the eutectic material very smooth, but the brass and steel were still gouged from machining and grinding. The hardness difference between the materials made the process difficult, but the only important material for analysis is the eutectic, meaning scratches in the surrounding materials are acceptable. In order to analyze the eutectic composition of the eutectic trigger, the material was etched. Initial assumptions of a lead-tin alloy proved to be wrong, as the material did not respond to any of the acid etchants tested, Nitric and Hydrochloric acid. After the eutectic alloy was identified, consulting the Metals Handbook indicated that electrolytic polishing with Nitric acid would reveal the grain structure. After the current was applied for 15 seconds the Bismuth was highly corroded, preferentially etched by the acid.

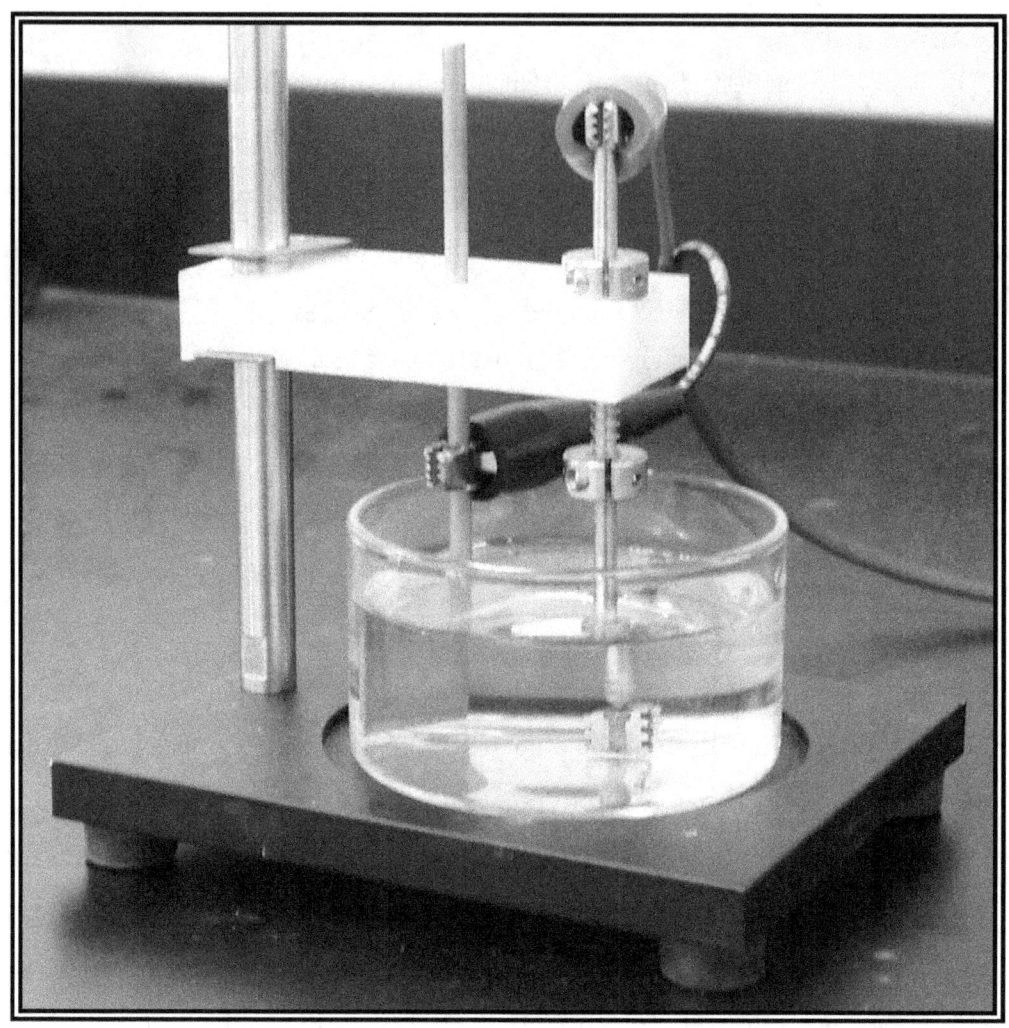

Fig 4.1 - Electrolytic Polishing apparatus with Eutectic Trigger

After etching, the sectioned eutectic trigger was viewed using an optical microscope to analyze the grain structure. The material consists of evenly dispersed Lead and Bismuth grains with a regular size or roughly 10μm, [Fig 4.2, 4.3]. This structure indicates the majority of the material is of eutectic composition, however it is impossible to perfectly determine the composition without a microprobe analysis. Elsewhere there is evidence that the material is off eutectic. Several large particles have remained un-etched [Fig 4.4, 4.5], suggesting that the composition leans more towards Lead, moving the composition off the eutectic point. The thermal analysis performed in Section 6 confirms this determination.

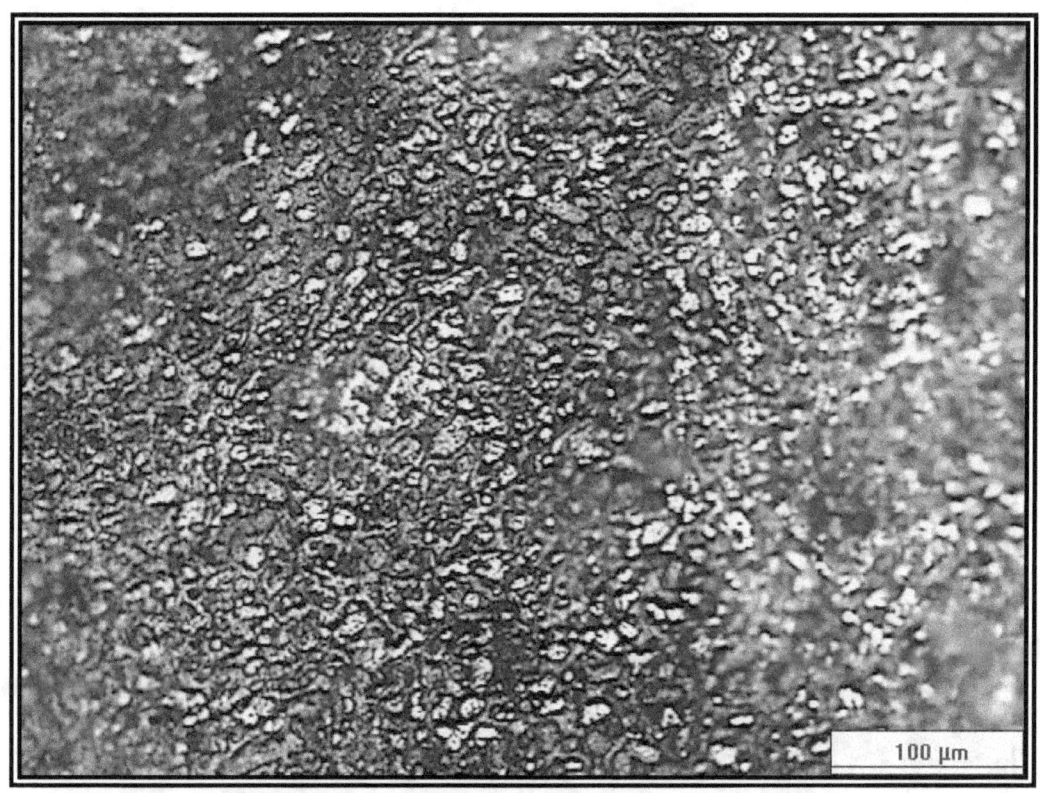

Fig 4.2 - Eutectic Material Grain Structure

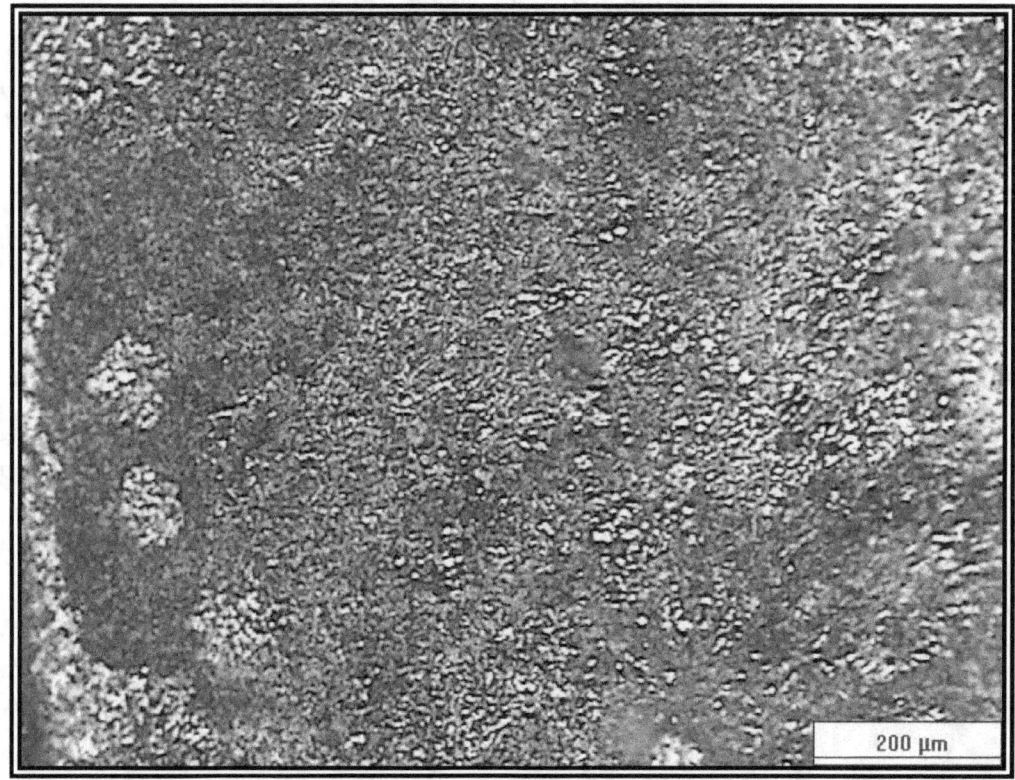

Fig 4.3 - Bismuth-Lead Eutectic Imbalance

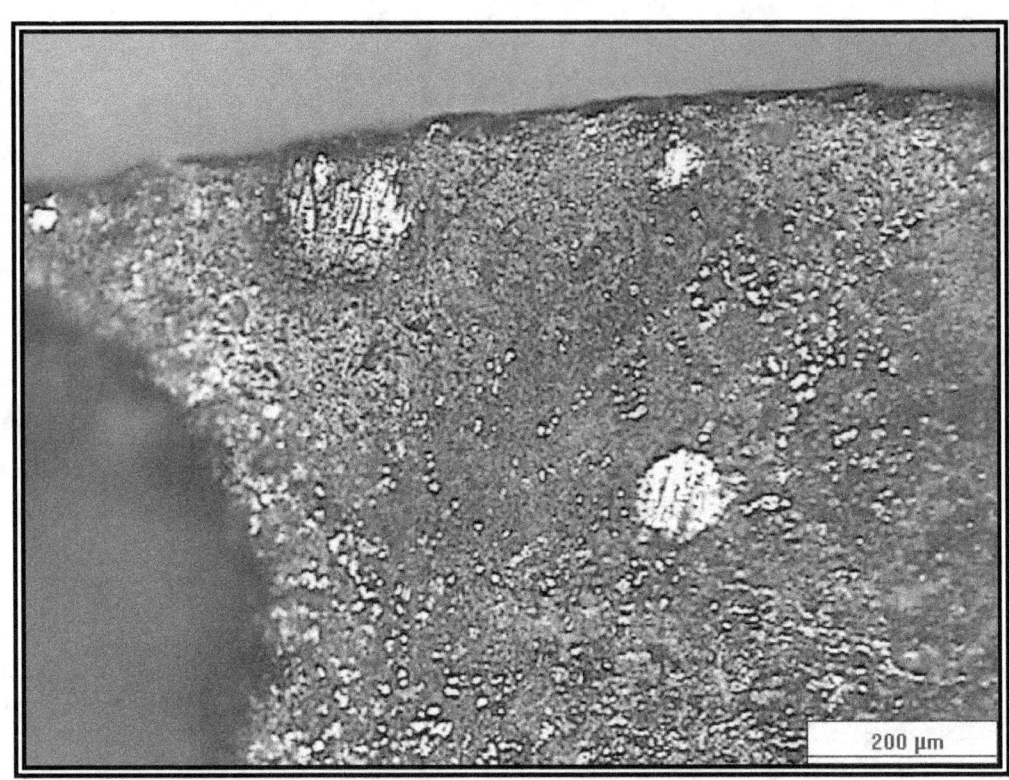

Fig 4.4 - Particles of Lead suspended in Eutectic

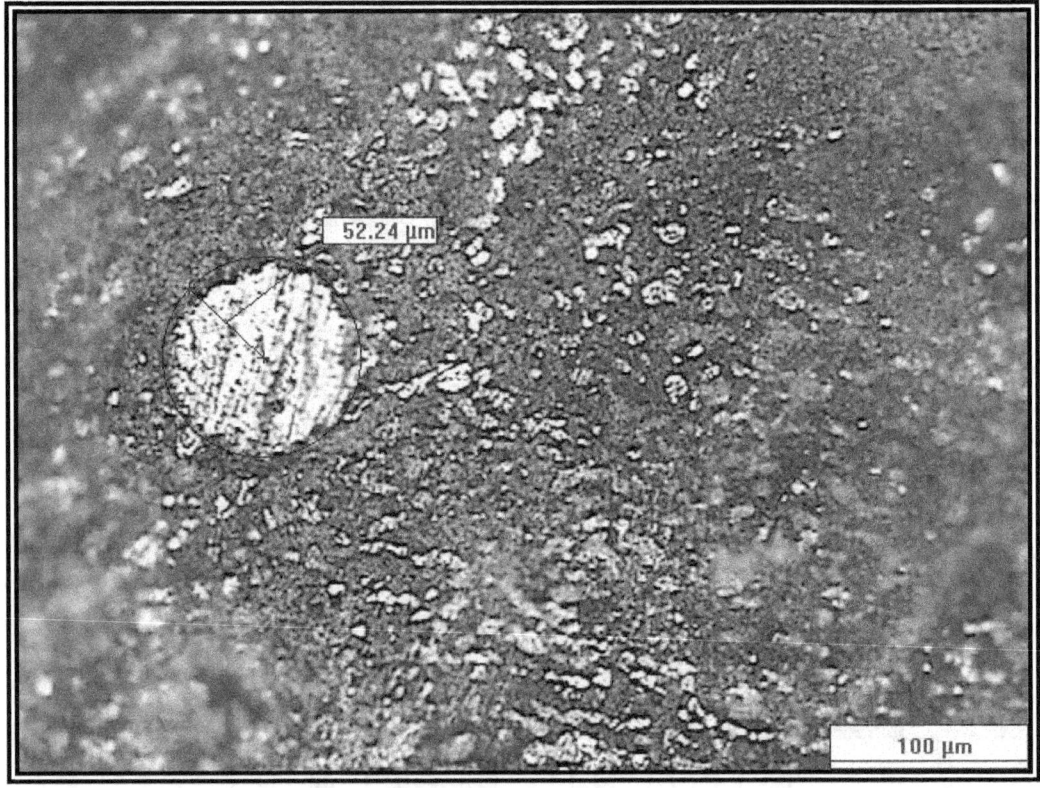

Fig 4.5 - Large Single Lead particle under close inspection

5. Thermal Profile

In order to verify the metallurgical analysis, a thermal profile was developed. It was obtained using a thermocouple inserted into two small holes drilled in the eutectic trigger core. The eutectic material was contained by a brass casting, which had been crimped at the bottom and sealed using aluminum foil to prevent leaking.

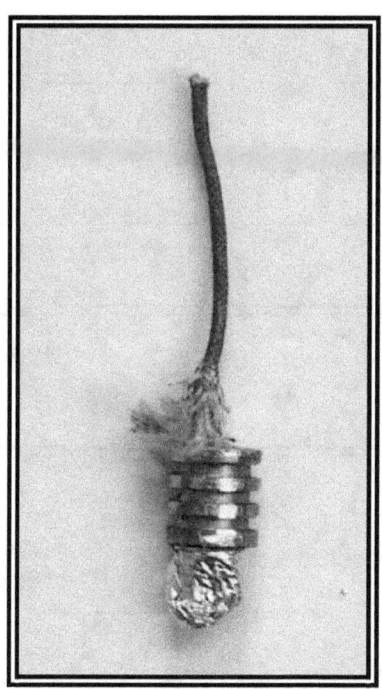

Fig 5.1 - Thermocouple inserted into eutectic trigger mechanism

The temperature was recorded using a very accurate National Instruments E-series DAQ board (NI PCI-6024E), using an SCXI thermocouple signal-conditioning unit (SCXI-1112). The temperature was sampled at a rate of 1 Hz while the trigger was inserted into an oven at 200°C, allowed to reach 150°C, and then removed and allowed to cool. The process was repeated for three trigger assemblies, all composed of the same eutectic material. Two triggers were from the Mirada PRD S/N 10416 that already had been disassembled; the third trigger was removed from Mirada PRD S/N 10420.

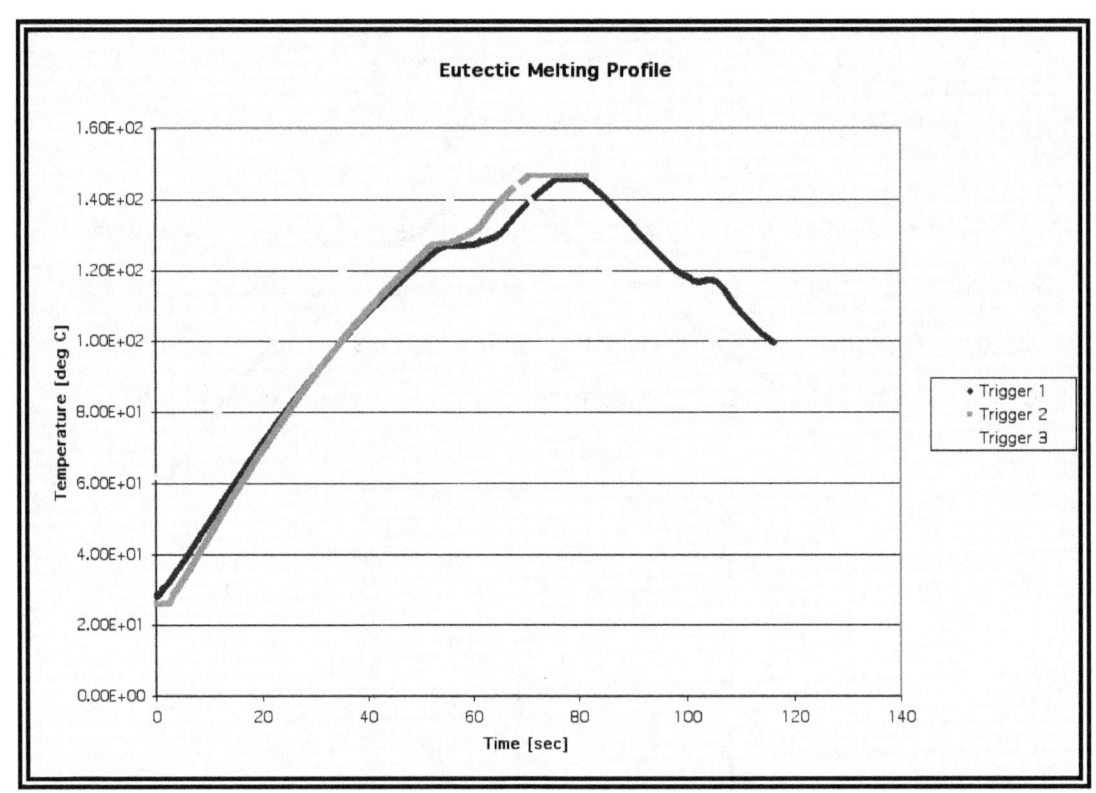

Fig 5.2 - Temperature Profile Plots of Eutectic Triggers

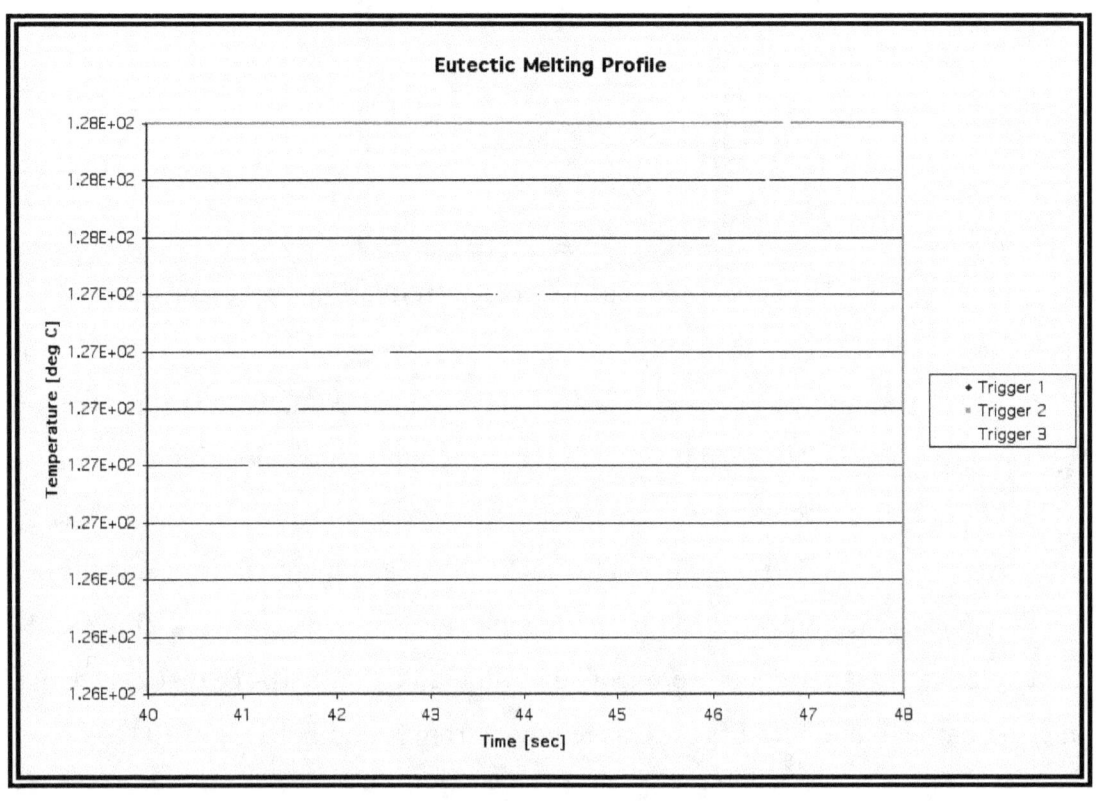

Fig 5.3 - Phase Change Plateau of Trigger 1

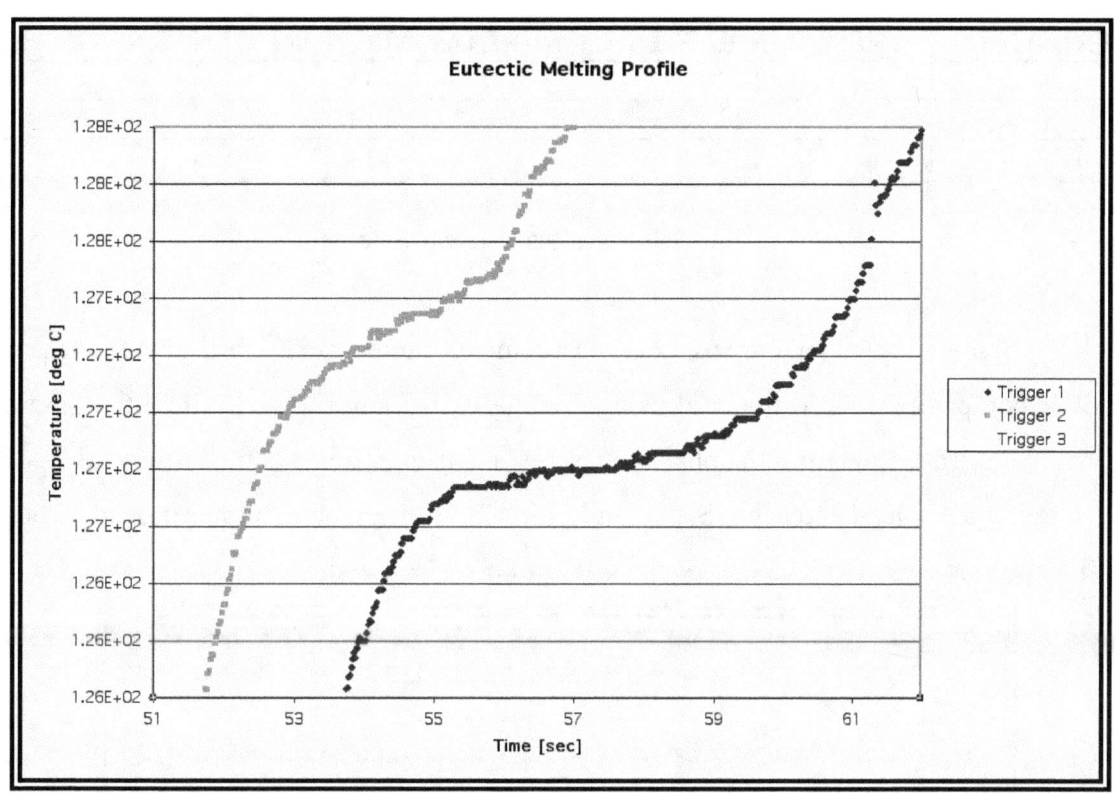

Fig 5.4 - Phase Change Plateau of Triggers 2 & 3

The thermal profile plots shown in Figures 5.2-5.4 show time on the x-axis against temperature on the y-axis. Figure 5.2 shows the entire thermal profile during heating, melting, cooling and solidification, Figures 5.3 and 5.4 only show the melting profiles of the plots for closer inspection. The phase transition during melting of all three triggers was investigated instead of the solidification phase transition as the melting data allows for easier and superior analysis, the cooling curves were discarded.

Analysis of the melting thermal profiles supports the theory that the material is off eutectic. The first trigger begins to melt at 127°C, remains at that temperature before the slope becomes steeper after four seconds, and then completes the phase transformation at 131°C, which indicates that the eutectic material melts first, followed by the melting of the off eutectic material. Triggers 2 and 3 have more slope during their melting stage, each beginning to melt at 127°C and completing the phase transformation at 133°C.

TRIGGER	INITIAL MELT T [°C]	FINAL MELT T [°C]	RANGE [°C]
1	127	131	4
2	127	133	6
3	127	133	6

Fig 5.5 - Melt Plateau Measurements

These melt plateau temperature measurements can be used to estimate the true eutectic composition of the material using the Phase diagram, shown in Fig 5.6. Reading the temperature ranges from the phase diagram gave trigger one a composition 1.3 % off eutectic higher in lead and triggers two and three 2.0% off eutectic higher in lead. The composition is close to the specified 45% Bismuth - 55% Lead.

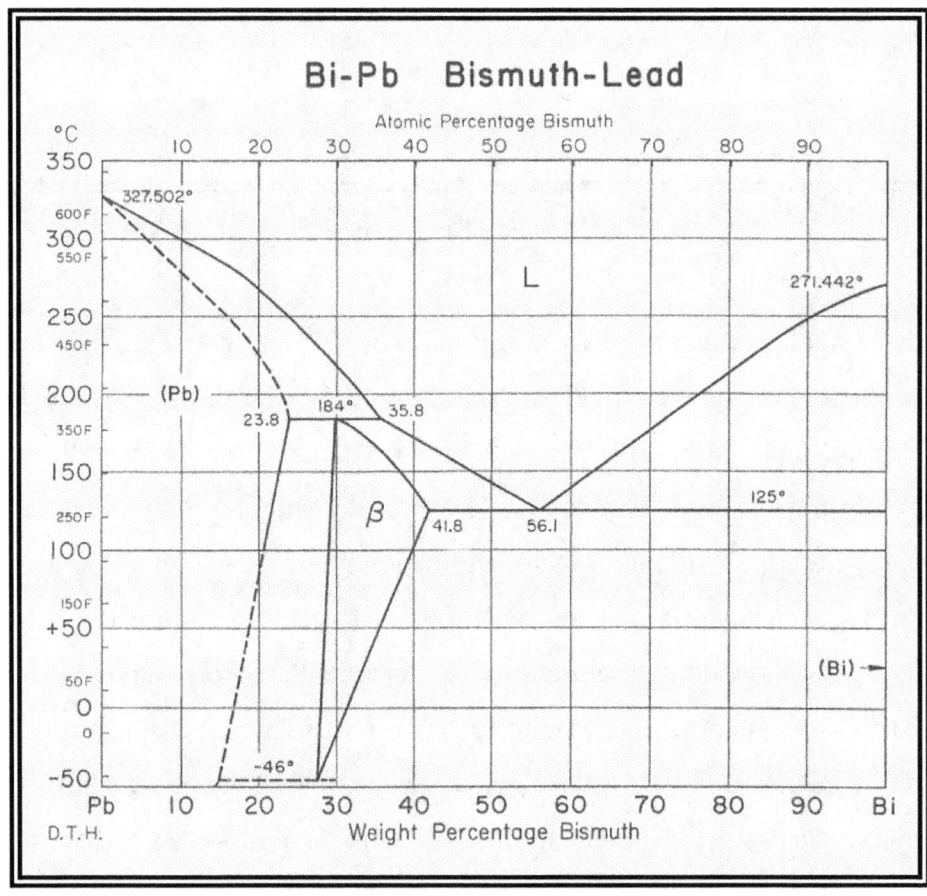

Fig 5.6 - Phase Diagram of Bismuth-Lead

6. Geometry and Forces

The spring-loaded bayonet that punctures the safety disc is held in place by two ball bearings, located at the bottom of each eutectic trigger. Therefore, each trigger is subject to some resultant vertical force from the spring. By measuring this force, it is possible to determine the chances of creep or plastic deformation as well as predict the effect of the casting voids.

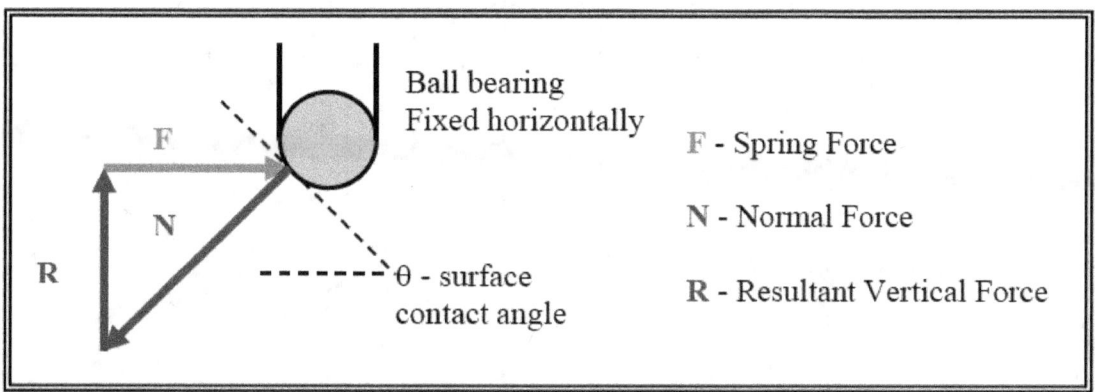

Fig 6.1 - Ball bearing static force diagram

6.1. Constriction Angle Calculation

The eutectic material was melted out of the sectioned trigger mechanism and the resulting void was measured with a set of venire calipers. Because of the poor surface finish and dimensional tolerances of the casting, dimensions were only taken to 0.01 in, but the ball bearing allowed accurate measurement, being a precision made part. The resulting geometry is shown in Figure 6.2. Basic trigonometry was used to determine the angles of the constricted sections of the trigger.

$$\alpha := \operatorname{atan}\left(\frac{0.03}{0.09}\right) \qquad \alpha = 18.435 \cdot \deg$$

$$\beta := \operatorname{atan}\left(\frac{0.08}{0.10}\right) \qquad \beta = 38.66 \cdot \deg$$

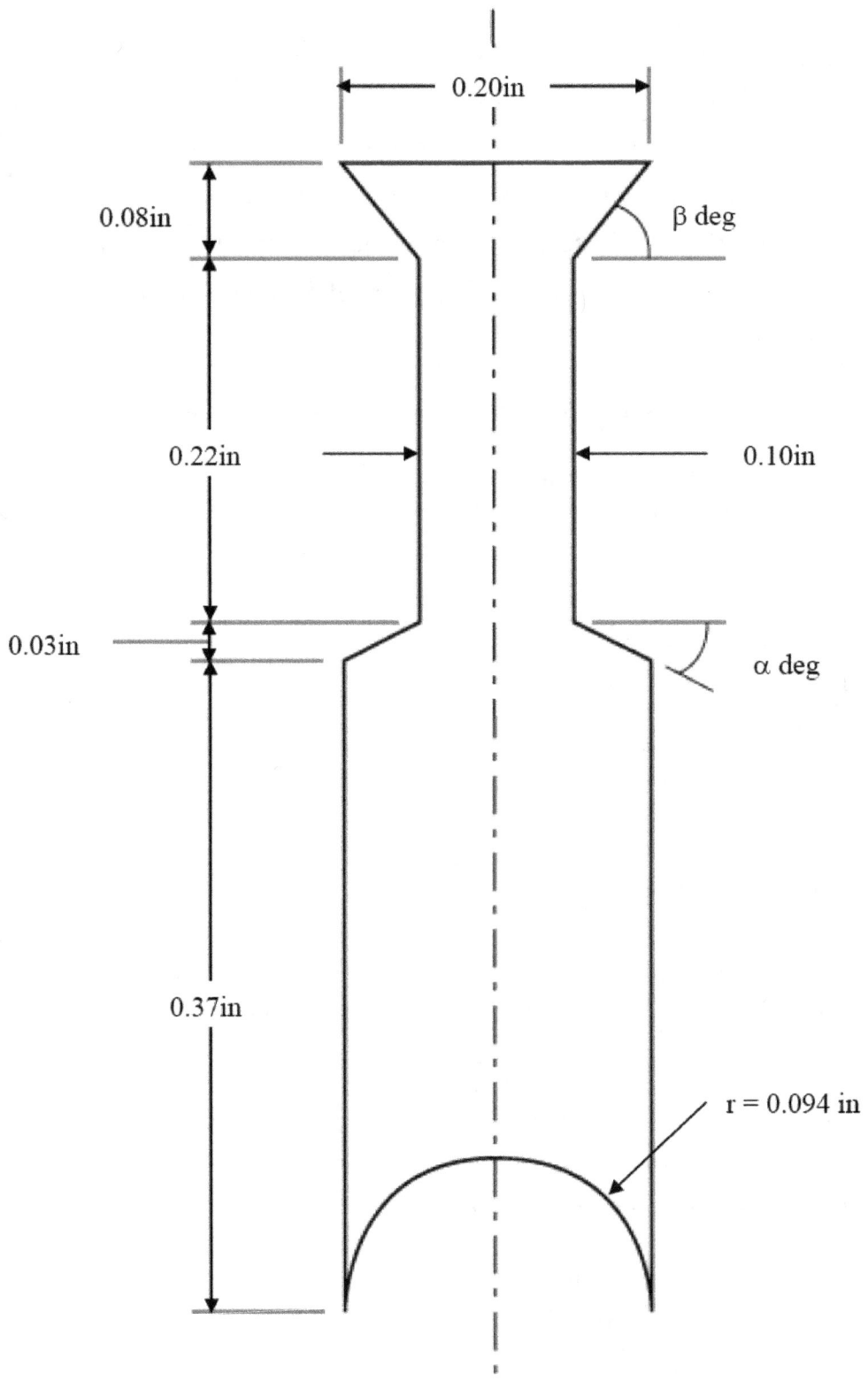

Fig 6.2 - PRD Trigger Geometry

6.2. Ball Bearing Contact Angle

By measuring the disassembled PRD with the triggers in place, measurement and calculation were made to determine the angle of contact between the bayonet and the ball bearing.

$$D_{Ball} := 0.188$$

$$r := \frac{D_{Ball}}{2} \qquad r = 0.094$$

$$y(x) := r - \sqrt{r^2 - x^2}$$

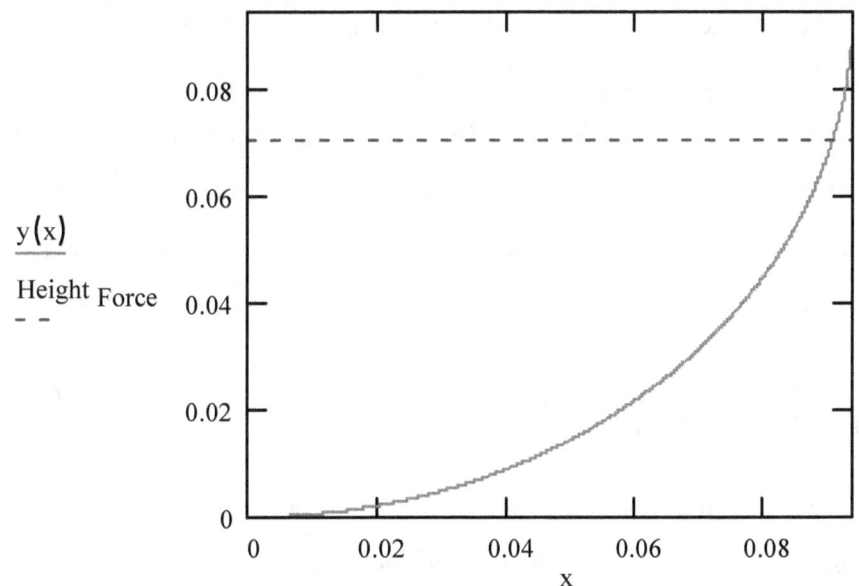

Given

$$y(x) = Height_{Force}$$

$$x_{contact} := Find(x) \qquad\qquad x_{contact} = 0.091$$

$$Angle_{Contact} := atan(dy(x_{contact})) \qquad \boxed{Angle_{Contact} = 75.208 \cdot deg}$$

6.3. Spring Constant

The spring used in the Mirada PRD is nearly fully compressed while installed. The spring was removed and its constant measured using an Instron stress analysis machine. The force was measured at the same compression level as installed in the PRD instead of measuring a spring constant. At the given level of compression, it is likely that the spring constant would become nonlinear. At a compression of 0.815 inches the spring exerted a force of 72.77 pounds.

6.4. Resultant Vertical Force

Because the ball bearing contacts the bayonet at an angle, there is a resultant vertical force acting on the eutectic material, shown diagrammatically in Fig 6.1. The spring force was calculated previously, and using basic trigonometry a force of 9.60 pounds per trigger was calculated, resulting in a pressure of 346 psi. Indium, the manufacturer of the eutectic material, specifies a yield stress of 6,400 psi, giving a shear stress of 3,200 psi, using Distortion Energy Theory (Mohrs Circle). The resulting shear stress on the eutectic material is around one tenth of is failing stress and the material is, therefore, not at risk of failure.

6.5. Void Shear Reduction Effect

The presence of large casting voids in the upper portion of the eutectic material could reduce the amount shear force required to move it, if a given void was closed instead of displacing the material above it. This effect was investigated by calculating the amount of surface contact area lost by the constricted area in the trigger, plotted in Fig 6.3. The x-axis is the radius of the void, the y-axis the surface area reduction ratio, calculated as the amount of surface sheared over a no void condition. A worst-case scenario is assumed in which the void is located as low as possible at the neck where the constricted area widens. If the eutectic material flows into the void, the equivalent volume of material does not have to be sheared along the walls, resulting in less force being required. Other scenarios investigated were having the void at different heights above the neck area. In these cases, more material would have to be sheared, as material under the void would have to be displaced. If a ratio greater than one is required, the void would not collapse, and the material would flow as if there were no void present. Results from this calculation show that even in the worst-case scenario, a ratio of 0.7 is obtained, which is still more than enough resistance to stop the eutectic material from moving.

$$H := 0.22 \qquad V_T := \pi \cdot R^2 \cdot H \qquad V_V(r) := \frac{4}{3} \cdot \pi \cdot r^3$$

$$h_r(r) := \frac{V_T - V_V(r)}{\pi \cdot R^2} \qquad \tau_{Ratio}(r, h) := \frac{h_r(r) \cdot R + r \cdot h}{H \cdot R}$$

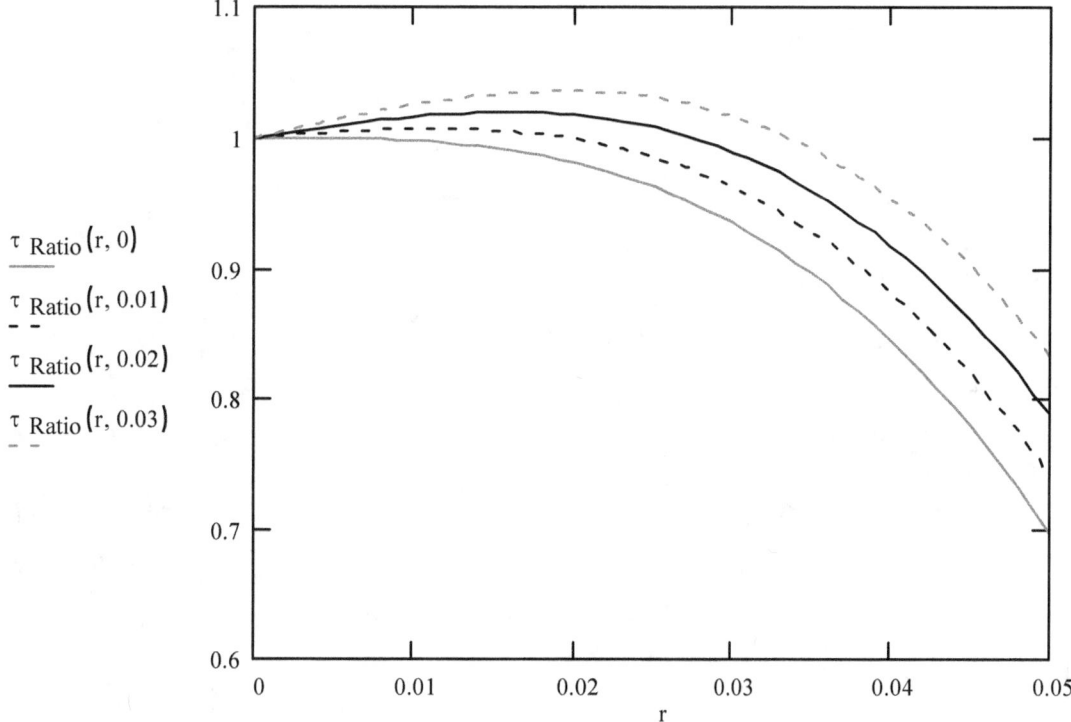

$\tau_{Ratio}(r, 0)$

$\tau_{Ratio}(r, 0.01)$

$\tau_{Ratio}(r, 0.02)$

$\tau_{Ratio}(r, 0.03)$

Fig 6.3 - Surface Area Reduction Ratio Plot

6.6. Upper Bound Hodogram

The resistance to the flow of the eutectic material comes form the constriction in the channel located halfway from the bottom. The eutectic material acts as a Bingham solid, plastically deforming and flowing like a thick paste similar to an extrusion process. This flow is complicated and difficult to calculate, but an upper bound analysis is possible. Using the principle of conservation of mass, a hodogram is constructed, and with knowledge of the system geometry, an equivalent shear stress can be computed. The hodogram is a two-dimensional analysis of plastic flow through a constriction, computing the pressure required to force material flow. Multiplying this pressure by two gives the pressure required to flow thorough a symmetrical planar constriction, and multiplying by four gives a low estimate for flow though a cylindrical constriction.

$$S_y := 6400$$

$$\tau_{xy} := 3200$$

$$\alpha = 18.435 \cdot deg$$

Inlet / Outlet Ratio $= 1.9$

$$\theta := 90 \cdot deg - \alpha \qquad\qquad \theta = 71.565 \cdot deg$$

$$W := 4 \cdot \left(\tan(\theta) + \frac{1}{1.9 \cdot \sin(\theta) \cdot \cos(\theta)} \right) \cdot \tau_{xy}$$

$$\boxed{W = 6.086 \cdot 10^4}$$

This low estimate gives a shear force requirement over 60,000 psi; the 360 psi acting on the eutectic material is less than five percent of this value. This calculation indicates that creep is unlikely. However, the analysis is not final until continued by physical experimentation.

7. Conclusions

The study indicates that the performance of the eutectic triggers is not going to be affected by the presence of the detected flaws in the eutectic material. The material has been shown to be only slightly off eutectic in composition. However, this would not change the melting temperature as to affect the triggering temperature. The melting process will take longer, on the order of seconds, and increase the viscosity of the molten eutectic during phase change compared to a perfect eutectic trigger. The delay could affect the performance of the PRD during a fire, but as vehicle fires are much hotter than the eutectic melting temperature, it is unlikely to cause the PRDs to fail to trigger in the time necessary for protecting the cylinder. The melting temperatures measured are all within a few degrees of the specified temperature of 123.8°C, showing the PRDs would have functioned correctly in the case of a fire.

Calculations determined that trigger failure from the detected voids and other defects is not a concern. Casting flaws are a very frequent occurrence. However, their presence is restricted to the upper portion of the trigger in the analyzed PRDs. It has been shown that the material properties and trigger geometry do not allow a big enough void for material shearing forces to become a concern **PRD failure is most likely a result of improper maintenance, including the well-documented water freezing problem, and/or a severe manufacturing defect[1].** The design itself is robust, and tolerant to minor defects and flaws. While a limited number of PRDs were evaluated, the principles discussed in this paper are applicable to the other PRDs used in natural gas transit bus service.

The upper bound hodogram calculations indicate that material creep or plastic deformation is highly unlikely at room temperatures because of the small force applied and large resistance to material flow. No evidence, actual or theoretical, exists to attribute PRD failure to creep. Plastic deformation remains a concern during the life of a PRD. The PRDs can reach 90 percent of the absolute melting temperature on a hot day during a fast fill. At this temperature the material properties can change dramatically

---

[1] No commentary or determination is made on the PRDs design for manufacturability, which should reduce the complexity of and probability for a manufacturing defect.

from those at room temperature where the eutectic material was originally characterized, and severe softening of the metal occurs. The eutectic material may have softened substantially, thus allowing plastic deformation to occur even under the relatively low loads applied within the PRD. However, there are currently no data classifying temperature dependent yield or shear strength for this material, and the matter requires further investigation.

8. Future

It has been hypothesized that eutectic creep could be responsible for PRD failure. So far, this has been the only phenomenon, independent of damage caused by freezing water, which is continually checked on active PRDs. In proper transit service operation, the PRD is removed upon suspicion of material creep. Because of the time scale required for a creep analysis, it was not tested in this initial investigation, only checked for in the PRD's analyzed. A potential future experiment will determine the amount of eutectic creep in the triggers by exposing test triggers to a constant pressure as seen in use, and to high temperature close to the melting temperature. By measuring the material displacement at different time intervals for several temperatures, a family of curves may be generated, providing insight into the last failure possibility for these triggers. Measuring the material properties of the eutectic at elevated temperatures using an Instron tensile test machine will allow for more accurate creep and plastic deformation calculations. By completing both creep calculations and experiments; a comparison is possible to determine the validity of the calculations. Previous investigations have failed to fully and correctly identify the failure mechanism. Additional insight into the failure modes was gained, but additional evaluation in needed. By fully identifying the failure mechanisms, proper design and manufacturing process control requirements could be implemented, both in practice and in standards requirements, to reduce the rate of failure of future PRDs.

9. References -

1. "Metals Handbook, 8th Edition", <u>American Society for Metals</u>, 1973
2. "Analysis of Mirada PRD Serial Number 10346", <u>Battelle</u>, February 22, 2002
3. "1997 Failure Rate Data - CNG Transit Busses (US)", <u>SAIC</u>, 1998
4. "Design and Materials Issues for PRDs for Natural Gas Vehicle Fuel Containers", <u>Gas Research Institute</u>, April 1998
5. "Performance Testing of Pressure Relief Devices for NGV Cylinders", <u>Gas Research Institute</u>, June 1997
6. "Mechanical Metallurgy", <u>McGraw-Hill, Inc.</u>, 1988
7. "Industrial Principles of Ceramic Processing", J.S. Reed
8. "APTA Public Transportation Factbook", <u>APTA</u>, 2003
9. "Principles of Materials Science and Engineering, Third Edition", William F. Smith, <u>McGraw-Hill, Inc.</u>, 1996